Plum Island Recollections

BE · JUST · AND · FEAR · NOT ·

Maddock

Plum Island Recollections

Views and Reminiscences of
Life on Plum Island c. 1900

Recounting the Deeds of

Capt. Thomas J. Maddock & the Crew of the

US Merrimack River Life Saving Station,

Plum Island, Massachusetts

by Vincent L. Wood

Merrimack River Life Saving Station crew launching a surf boat in heavy sea to go out to a wreck in a storm at Plum Island, 1910.

All photographs in this book were taken by Gardner Perry Wood.

Printed & Published by
Newburyport Press, Inc., Newbury, MA
First printing, November, 1995

ISBN 1-882266-04-8

Cover Photo: Captain Thomas J. Maddock in boathouse annex, 1905. Fire buckets overhead.

DEDICATION

This book is dedicated to the Maddock and Wood boys who served faithfully as volunteers at the U.S. Merrimack River Life Saving Station Plum Island, MA during the summer months of the early years of the twentieth century.

ACKNOWLEDGEMENTS

Although no longer with us, I gratefully acknowledge the many people who told me the stories contained in this book: Captain Thomas J. Maddock, his son Ralph, my grandfather Gardner Perry Wood, who took all the pictures, my grandmother Laura Wood, my father Ralph C. Wood, my mother Marion E. Wood, my uncles Wilbur LeRoy Wood, John Bertram Wood, and Leon R. Wood. Thanks to Ruth Adam, the Captain's granddaughter. And thanks also to Nancy Weare for her encouragement, advice, and verification of subjects of which I was unsure, to Todd Woodworth for his assistance, and to the Newburyport Library for helping me verify dates and other information.

A very special thanks to my wife, Hope G. Wood, who transcribed my manuscript, written in longhand, to her computer. If it were not for her invaluable assistance and cooperation this publication would not have been possible.

PREFACE

As a child and teenager I was fascinated to listen to the talk going on around me from my parents, grandparents, and uncles, especially Uncle Tom Maddock, my grand-mother Wood's brother. I loved to hear about the surf boats, the breeches buoy, the bucket brigades, and most of all, the stories about the Island in the old days. For some reason, I felt compelled, at an early age, to jot down little notes about things I saw and heard. These notes and the many photographs of my grandfather's are the basis of this publication.

Every summer, while staying with my family at the Elora cottage, I constantly roamed the Island. I mentally noticed the names of all the cottages as I went. There were not a tenth of the number of cottages then as now. Oh! that I had written all their names down, along with their locations; or that I could remember them all. In those days the road from the center to the south, now called Southern Boulevard, terminated in a large round parking lot known as the circle. It was located about where the parking lot is now, at the end of Southern Boulevard. There was yet another road, from there along the banks of the Plum Island River going south. It was little more than two ruts, strewn with clam shells and sole leather scraps from Newburyport's many shoe shops. It was passable for the autos of the more daring, between tides, as far south as Grape Island. The ruts were filled with water in many places at low tide, and completely under water at high tide. After lingering too long before starting back, many an adventurer found themselves, much to their dismay, stranded with the water above their running boards. In the summer of 1937, after equipping my 1935 V8 Ford with oversized tires, I made the trip many times. However, during the following winter, my entire exhaust system rusted away from the action of the salt water.

Loving the Island as I do, and being in possession of dozens of my grandfather's photographic glass plate negatives, along with a wealth of notes and memories, I decided to put it all together in one book. If anyone is able to identify people unnamed in these photos, please contact me.

Captain Thomas J. Maddock in civilian attire in boathouse annex of U.S. Merrimack River Life Saving Station at Plum Island, circa 1910.

AT THIS WRITING, there are few people alive who remember Capt. Maddock of the U.S. Life Saving Service at Plum Island, Massachusetts. In the 1920's and 1930's he was very visible. A man of medium height and weight, he meandered from place to place. His dark hair was shot with gray, his mustache all white. He was a very affable man who obviously enjoyed passing the time of day with everyone. Even when his expression was serious, his blue eyes had a twinkle. His favorite comment to describe a person in good spirits was, "He's as happy as a clam at high water." His quick wit and dry humor were priceless. In his seventies he still carried himself with proud military bearing.

1

Captain Maddock was the man everyone sought out to answer questions about the sea and the "Island" and all answers were freely given. Most of his life had been spent on the "Island". Keenly aware of all of nature's actions there, he had carefully observed and studied the impact the sea had on the "Island" in storm and calm. Though he had retired in 1919 he still spent much time at the station talking with the men and watching them at their duties.

John T. Maddock and wife, Katherine, at home in North Scituate, about 1890.

Thomas John Maddock was born in North Scituate, MA on August 8, 1859, the first son of John T. and Katherine Murdock Maddock. His father, John, was a seafaring man, born to a commission in the Royal Navy in Waterford County, Ireland, just across the water from Bristol, England. He ran away from home at the age of twelve after an altercation with his very stern father. He hastily signed on to an English ship as cabin boy and was at sea before he really had time to properly assess his situation. He landed in Boston where he obtained a berth on another ship which did not return for two years. It became his way of life. Voyage after voyage, some short, but most of long duration, many of them around the Horn. He served briefly aboard the U.S. Constitution. (Old Ironsides).

John married Katherine Murdock, who, although born in Bristol, did not meet John until she came to Boston. They established a home in North Scituate, Ma. shortly before the Civil War. He always intended return to Ireland and make amends, but procrastinated too long. The early death of his parents left him feeling "high and dry" as he put it. It put a sadness in his heart that never left him. He often cautioned his children, "Guard your temper well, for mine has cost me dearly!" After two daughters, Jennie L. and Laura M., John and Catherine had another son, Alonzo

Captain Maddock's sisters: Jennie Maddock, left, and Laura Maddock, right.

The children looked forward to their father's return from his long voyages. He always had little souvenirs from foreign ports hidden away in his ditty bag. When the time was near for his arrival, Laura would shinny up the flag pole where she could see her father turn down the lane toward the house. When he appeared she would slide to the ground and race up the lane to be the first to greet him. He would catch her in his arms as she leaped toward him. Long before the children grew up, John tired of the long periods away from his family. Giving up the sea, he spent the rest of his active years as a Boston Harbor pilot. The children all remembered the messenger in the middle of the night tossing pebbles against the window pane and calling "John Maddox - John Maddox - a ship is in" His children remember the messenger pronouncing his name as though it ended with an "x". He was on call twenty four hours a day to pilot ships through the tricky waters between the islands to the docks.

On March 1, 1887, when he was twenty seven, Thomas enlisted in the United States Life Saving Service. which later became the United States Coast Guard. After serving at the North Scituate Life Saving Station for ten years he assumed command of the Merrimack River Life Saving Station at Plum Island in 1897. Tom was married to Florence Cushman. They had six children, five boys and a girl: Richie, Willard, Ralph, Jay, Ruth, and John.

Old Scituate Lighthouse at Scituate Harbor, as it appeared in 1890.

Photo at right: Thomas J. Maddock at age 30 while serving at the Life Saving Station, North Scituate, Massachusetts, 1890.

Photo below: Tom Maddock and family at the Life Saving Station, in the boathouse annex.
Left to right in front: Ralph and Jay
Left to right in the rear: Tom holding Ruth, Willard, Richie, and Florence holding John.

During the summer months, the regular crew at the station was off duty, as most of the serious rescue work was needed in the bad weather months. Even so, in the summer, there were still many emergencies caused by thunderstorms, and foggy weather. Pleasure craft and amateur fishermen were also often in trouble, and swimmers were caught in the tricky currents and undertow. The populace also relied heavily on the Life Saving Service for help at fires. In times of emergency Tom sought the help of volunteers and friends.

Photo at right: Merrimack River Life Saving Station at Plum Island as it appeared in 1897 when Captain Maddock assumed command there.

Below: Capt. Maddock with a St. Bernard dog in the doorway of the boathouse annex. The boathouse, which was previously the station, is seen at the left.

The front of Merrimack River Life Saving Station after the addition of the front porch. Signal flaps are flying in honor of Independence Day - the Fourth of July - c. 1905.

Merrimack River Life Saving Station compound looking north, c. 1910. Privy on left, little boathouse on the right. The boathouse, which was previously the station house, was moved there from High Sandy in 1881. The boathouse still stands today, converted to a dwelling at its original site on 45th street. The station house was built in 1890.

Photo above: Left to right, Laura Mae Wood, Ruth Maddock, and Helen Wood, c. 1908. Below: Captain Maddock with Ruth and John, ages 8 and 6, on the ramp of the boathouse annex.

The wreck of the Jennie M. Carter at Salisbury Beach. Photo taken April 14, 1894.

Capt. Maddock with his four youngest children in the boathouse, Left to right: Ruth, John, Ralph, and Jay in the rear.

Above: The Wood boys at 80 School Street, Groveland, Massachusetts in 1910.
Left to right: J. Bertram (Ted), Wilbur LeRoy (Roy), Ralph, and Leon in the rear.
Below: Merrimack River Life Saving Station compound viewed from the shore
looking northwest, c. 1905.

By 1905, Captain Maddock's boys were a big help to him in the summertime, as were the boys of his sister, Laura Wood, the writer's grandmother. As soon as school was out, Laura and her four sons, Roy, Ted, Ralph and Leon, would come down the river from Groveland to stay at the station. Laura helped Florence with the cooking and household chores, while the boys applied themselves to station duties, along with their Maddock Cousins.

The Wood family on the veranda at 80 School Street, Groveland, MA, c. 1915.
Left to right: in front, Gardner, in the middle, Ted and Leon, and in the rear,
Ralph (on the railing), Laura, and Roy.

Before the regular crew left for the summer, Captain Maddock would send a surf boat up the river to Groveland on the incoming tide. The Wood family would load all their gear and clothing, then climb aboard. Then they would catch the outgoing tide, riding it down river to the Plum Island Basin. Everything aboard had to be carried over the sand to the station, which was located out on the shore at what is now 45th Street. The boat was then taken out the mouth of the Merrimack around to the station.

Laura's husband, Gardner Perry Wood, my grandfather, would come down to the Island on the street car for weekends and holidays. He would always bring his camera. The pictures in this publication were taken by him. He did all his own developing and printing, an art he taught me when I was in my early teens.

Laura Maddock Wood at Plum Island jetty 1915.

The photographer who took the photos in this publication, Gardner Perry Wood, with his wife Laura Maddock Wood in the garden of their home at 80 School Street, Groveland, MA, in 1920. Holding the rubber shutter bulb in his right hand, Gardner is taking this photo himself.

80 School Street, Groveland, MA,
Home of Gardner Perry Wood and his wife Laura Maddock Wood.
Taken on Decoration Day (Memorial Day) in 1915.

Captain Maddock held regular drills for the Maddock and Wood boys in the summer just as he did with the regular crew the rest of the year. They held drills in bucket brigade as well as surf boat, and breeches buoy work. By 1908 the summer crew was as proficient as the winter crew.

Surf boat drill in front of the Merrimack River Life Saving Station, 1909.

Capt. Maddock in the annex, seated in front of the surf-boat. Note cork life preservers hanging over the boat, lyle gun projectiles at the far left, and two breeches buoy reels on carts in center.

Richie Maddock at 80 School Street, Groveland,
MA at age 18, shortly after joining the U.S. Navy.

Through the participation of the two families the lookout tower was manned from dawn to dusk, the patrols were made, and emergencies were covered. I do not know if there was any monetary remuneration to the boys for duties performed or not. The station was like a social center in those days. The boys on duty managed to have a good time on the beach. It was there that my mother and father met.

Willard Maddock in front of the boat house annex at age 14.

Jay Maddock at the left, Ralph Maddock at the right, at the back door of 80 School Street, Groveland. When this photo was taken, Jay was 9 and Ralph 6 years of age.

In 1897 my mother's father Frank M. Worthen, who was the Town of Groveland's first U.S. Mail letter carrier, built the Elora Cottage on one of the most desirable lots on the Island. It was located on the sea shore where the basin is at it's closest point to the ocean, still standing with a large addition at 100 Northern Boulevard. As was the case with most of the cottages on the Island, the building materials had been brought down river from Haverhill on a barge. My mother, only five years of age at the time, made the trip and told me about the experience. She remembered getting aboard in Groveland and making the trip down river. They spent the night tied up in Newburyport so they could catch the tide right, to bring the barge into the point the next day. She recalled falling asleep beneath the deck of the barge listening to the men talking on the deck above. She watched the lumber being transferred from the barge to the "Dummy", then the ride on the "Dummy" to the site of the Elora.

Photos on this page, at top:
Storm damage to Plum Island cottages, c. 1910.
Photo below: Looking toward Blackrocks,
Salisbury from station tower. Unidentified cottage.

Previous page, photo at top: The Elora cottage, summer
home of the writer's mother, Marian Worthen Wood.
Photo at bottom: Little boathouse from station tower.
Weather vane on the post at left.

The cottage was typical of Plum Island summer cottages of that period, a storey and a half, l8' x 24', resting on cedar posts, board and batten siding, with a roofed piazza on four sides. The piazza roof was primarily for protection from the sun rather than rain, although by my time, it had been covered with heavy tar paper. It had a chimney which rested on a pedestal attached to the floor frame. Inside was a living room, dining room, and kitchen on the first floor, and four bedrooms on the second. In the kitchen was a black iron range and a pitcher pump splashed water into a black iron sink. A three burner kerosene cook stove was used if there was no fire in the range. A large oval, ornate, stained glass chandelier-type kerosene lamp hung over the drop leaf dining table. A homemade ice chest stood in a corner of the dining room. There was a foot pedal pump organ in the living room. A commode, complete with a wash bowl, pitcher and chamber pot stood beside the bed in each bedroom.

When there was a cold nor'easter storm, a coal fire was built in the kitchen range. I would be handed a coal hod and sent out to the shore. It would not take long to fill it with coal, which was plentiful along the shore. The coal came from the many wrecks of coal barges over the years.

The cottage was modernized with tube and post electrical wiring in 1922 by Uncle Ted, who had become one of the first electrical contractors in the area. A combination wood shed and out house privy could be found behind the house. The oceanside was considered the front. My mother and her many girl friends became acquainted with the Maddock and Wood boys, forming a sort of social group. They used the station and the Elora cottage as meeting places and could be found every Saturday night at the dance pavilion at the center.

Two or three times during each summer, just about dusk, the silver hake would wash ashore on the waves by the dozens. We would gather up enough for a fish fry. Being a very soft fish, they would not keep for more than a few hours, so they would be dressed and fried immediately. They were delicious. Uncle Tom told me the hake would chase the sand eels, which in those days were all along the shore in schools of hundreds. He said at certain times, when the moon and the tide were right, at dusk, the hake would follow the eels in so close to shore they would be caught in the surf and wash ashore. It has been many years since I have heard of this happening. I believe it is because most of the sand eels are gathered up in nets commercially for bait. I know

26

it has been a long time since I have experienced the tickling sensation of a school of sand eels passing around me as I stood in the surf. A very common experience when I was young.

The carefree days ended in 1916 with the marriage of my mother, Marian Worthen, to my father, Ralph Wood. In the same year, Berta Parker married Wilbur LeRoy (Roy) Wood. Annabelle Sawyer, Marion's best friend, married John Bertram (Ted) Wood and Louise Hauger, daughter of the Groveland Methodist Church's minister, married Leon Wood.

Photos on opposite page: Above, a three masted schooner being towed up the river by a tug. Below, the beach at Plum Island center. Bennett Hill cottage, formerly the Simpson cottage, is in the right background, c. 1900.

Photo at right: Wedding picture of Ralph and Marian Worthen Wood, the author's parents, in the garden of 80 School Street, Groveland, MA on June 20, 1916.

At about the same time Ethel King married Willard (Bill) Maddock. Inez Smith married Jay Maddock. Bessie Hopkinson married Ralph Maddock and Ruth Maddock married Walter Lothrop. Earlier, Ritchie Maddock joined the Navy, and John went with his mother when Florence and the Captain separated.

So the end of an era came swiftly. Once again it became necessary to solicit the services of volunteers. However, many of the boys spent weekends, from time to time, at the station and at the Elora with their new families. Most emergencies occurred weekends.

Photo below: The Maddock and Wood families at the station in 1902.

Left to right in front: Ted Wood, Leon Wood, Ruth Maddock, Tom Maddock with cello, Florence Maddock with banjo, Helen Wood with violin, Roy Wood with violin, Laura Mae Wood with mandolin. In the rear: Thomas Wood, Ralph Wood with ball, Richie Maddock, Jennie Maddock Wood, Laura Maddock Wood, and Roswell Wood, Mayor of Haverhill, 1904 - 1908.

*Top, Merrimack River Life Saving Station crew at breeches buoy drill on Plum Island, c. 1910.
Center, Victim in breech buoy during a drill in front of Merrimack River Life Saving Station,
Plum Island, c. 1910. Bottom, Merrimack River Station crew at breeches buoy drill, c. 1910.*

Breeches buoy drill being held in front of the station, c. 1910.
All the girls get into the act.

As a child I spent a good part of the summer at the Elora cottage with my mother and father, three younger sisters, and two younger brothers, Marjorie, Richard, Dorothy, Elizabeth, and David. I have sketchy recollections of riding over Plum Island bridge on the trolley car when I was very young. Just able to peek out the window, it terrified me to see nothing but water. It was also frightening to approach Plum Island Point on the trolley. Before coming to a stop at what seemed like the very edge of the water, looking out the front window of the car all I could see from my seat was the water coming closer and closer. When I voiced my fears, my mother showed me that the car could not reach the water because the tracks curved upward several feet at the end.

Original wooden bridge over Plum Island River.

I also remember seeing my father take the ice tongs, that hung by the chimney, out to the "Dummy" to bring back a large cake of ice to put in the ice chest. The "Dummy" was a sort of flat bed trolley car used to transport things from Newburyport, and from the Point to various places along its route. I believe this flat bed trolley car inherited the name "Dummy" from it's predecessor, the flat bed car with a dummy steam engine. Building materials for cottages came from the landing at the point to their sites on the "Dummy".

I recall overhearing discussions between my grandfather Worthen and the rest of the family as to whether or not they they had done the right thing to pay the Plum Island Beach Co. for the land on which the Elora stood. Cottage owners were given a choice of buying the land at the price the company set, or selling the cottage to the company for what they offered as a fair price. My grandfather maintained they offered too little for the cottage. He also said the lots were "too dang small". I remember hearing him saying "Mark my words, the time will come when there will be so many cottages on the Island it won't be a fit place to live." I also remember Uncle Tom's similar words to that effect. Little did they know how many cottages would become year-round dwellings, which at that time was unheard of.

A close relationship existed between the whole Wood family and Uncle Tom, as we called Captain Maddock. My father worked all week but was at the Island on the weekends. He spent a great deal of time visiting Uncle Tom at his new home, "Bonnyview" cottage, which he had built when he retired in 1919.

I used to beg to tag along. I was fascinated by the tales Uncle Tom told of days gone by. Many times Uncle Ted, Aunt Belle, and their daughter, Lois, were there also. As Lois's father was my father's brother, and her mother was my mother's best friend, the two families spent much time together. My grandparents were also frequent visitors at the "Bonnyview". Occasionally some of Uncle Tom's family would also be there.

Photo above: The view from station tower looking south, c. 1910. Minnie E. cottage is second from the right. The gambrel roof cottage left of center is the Beacon cottage.

On opposite page: an open electric trolley car on the bridge crossing the Artichoke River on its way to Newburyport, c. 1910.

From 1891 on, it was possible to travel from Groveland to Plum Island by trolley car. After 1922 the trolley at Plum Island was discontinued, the tracks torn up, and replaced with a road made of tar and sand nearly a foot thick. This road was so narrow, it was only by exercising extreme care that two autos were able to pass by each other, should they meet. The drifting sand spilled over the shoulders of the roadway in an uneven line making it difficult to tell where the edge was. It was not uncommon for the wheels of an auto to slip off into the sand and once this happened, it was impossible to get back on to the road surface. People from nearby cottages would come out with burlap bags and boards to place under the wheels. As the driver steered the auto, as many men as could get around it would push and practically lift it back on to the road.

At that time it was necessary to change from the trolley to a bus, at the Newburyport B & M railroad depot on Winter Street, to reach Plum Island. Ernest Boutin, and his brother, operated the Boutin Brothers Bus Company on a regular schedule: on the hour and half hour, from six in the morning until eleven at night, from the depot to Plum Island Point. The bus route was along Merrimack Street, up State Street, along High Street to Marlboro Street It went down Marlboro Street to Water Street and thence to Plum Island, by way of a wooden bridge crossing the Plum Island River.

During the years when the station was bustling with social activities, it was common to have sing-alongs. Uncle Tom played the cello and banjo, my grandfather Wood, with his sons Roy and Ralph, played violins. Florence Maddock played a banjo. My mother, Marian Worthen, played the mandolin as did Laura Mae Wood. Helen Wood played a violin and Ted Wood played drums. Ralph Wood also played a cornet. All the others sang. They would carry on for hours unless interrupted by an emergency. After a rescue all hands, men and women alike, would haul the surf boat back up the tracks into the boat house

Above: All hands pulling in the surfboat, c. 1910.

Opposite page. Top photo: On the station piazza in 1910. Left to right in front, Helen Wood MacSpadden, Laura Maddock Wood, Laura Mae Wood Ellis. In the middle, Jennie Maddock Wood, Tom Maddock, Gardner Perry Wood (book photographer) and in the rear, Leon Wood on the railing, John MacSpadden and Ted Wood.

Bottom photo: Clowning around at the Merrimack River station in 1910. John McSpadden with oar, Arthur Ellis, Helen Wood MacSpadden, Laura Mae Wood Ellis, Laura Maddock Wood, Leon Wood, Jennie Maddock Wood and Tom Maddock.

After refreshments, they would resume playing and singing. Occasionally a play would be performed under the direction of sister Laura Wood. Entertainment was sometimes also provided by Uncle Tom's niece, Laura Mae Wood., an elocution teacher, the daughter of Tom's sister Jennie, and Roswell L. (Ross) Wood, Mayor of Haverhill from 1904 to 1908. Uncle Tom's brother Lon, and his wife Nellie, were seldom around. He was the editor of a newspaper in St. Petersburg, Florida. They came for a two week vacation once a year. When a lot of the old crowd assembled at the "Bonnyview", it was the way they now describe the old days, with music and merriment on the porch. Lemonade and cookies were frequently served by Aunt Alice, Uncle Tom's new wife. He and Alice Hawthorne, from West Concord, New Hampshire were married shortly after his retirement in 1919. She was a very pretty, gracious lady, and everyone loved her.

On the porch were rugs made from departed Saint Bernard dogs. Their heads were stuffed and adorned with realistic, glass eyes. They all had names, usually taken from the Bible. The dog I remember most was one that was still alive, Ali Baba. His name, Uncle Tom told me, was inspired by the tale of " Ali Baba and the Forty Thieves," from "The Arabian Nights"

Merrimack River Life Saving Station before the front porch was added, c. 1900.
Left to right: Sitting, Jennie Wood, Laura Wood. Standing, Helen Wood, Laura Mae Wood.

Merrimack River Station crew with their families on the back porch of the station house, c. 1910.

Capt. Maddock is on the far right.

Below: Capt. Maddock and crew on the back porch of the station, c. 1910.

Uncle Tom had always kept two or three Saint Bernard dogs at the station. One accompanied the man on patrol in severe weather.. Another animal kept at the station, was "Inez" the horse. Inez was used primarily to haul the heavy cart of breeches buoy gear out to the shore when there was a drill or a wreck. When not needed for work, she was used to run errands or for pleasure rides, pulling a two wheel gig called the "Chariot". The Chariot had wide rimmed wheels for traveling in sand, and a good sized box in the rear for carrying objects or children. Inez's successor was allowed to run loose on the Island. On more than one occasion I recall women losing a pie or a pudding that had been put out to cool on their porch, to the horse. Numerous other times he became tangled in a line full of drying clothes. There were many complaints registered about him.

Laura Wood and son, Ralph, in the Chariot pulled by the station's horse, Inez, c. 1910. Hollis and Dorothy Waldo are in the rear. Two of the station's St. Bernard dogs at right.

When I was seven or eight, after pestering my mother incessantly, I was finally allowed to visit Uncle Tom by myself. I remember walking barefoot down the road. It felt so smooth. The tar road had been put in when they tore up the trolley car tracks. In the early summer before my feet toughened, it used to feel very hot in the middle of the day. Sometimes, the heat became unbearable and I would jump off the road, burrowing my feet deep into the sand where it was cooler. In my early teens the old tar road was replaced with macadam. I was very unhappy about this. The new road was very rough on my bare feet.

I was a welcome visitor at the Bonnyview.. Uncle Tom loved to tell stories about the Island, the Life Saving Station, and the old days. I was an avid listener. There were always cookies and milk or lemonade.

The Bonnyview cottage, Plum Island, Massachusetts, home of Tom and Alice Maddock after Tom's retirement, c. 1920. Below: Tom Maddock with banjo, and his wife, Alice, at home at the Bonnyview.. Maddock coat of arms hangs on the wall.

Uncle Tom told me about how terrible it was for men on patrol during winter storms. How it was impossible to stay on the shore with huge waves of icy water breaking well above the edge of the grass. Since it was required to stay as close to the water's edge as possible, the men were constantly in peril of getting caught by a wave as they scrambled up the side of a dune. If they became too wet they would be in danger of freezing to death before they reached the half way post at "High Sandy", or their own station on the way back. They usually took a dog along in case they got into trouble. He told of a time when the man on patrol did not return. Four men and the other dogs went out searching for him. They found him at High Sandy, soaking wet and barely conscious, huddled with the dog on the side of a dune. They carried him back to the station, where he was warmed up and put to bed. He caught pneumonia but survived.

He related another time when the wreck was so far out the projectile fell short each time they fired. They did not want to launch a boat because the sea was running so heavy but it seemed to be the only thing to do. Finally, when they were about to give up, the wind died down a little and the shot fell on board. The breeches buoy was rigged and all hands brought in safely. The ship broke up just as the last man reached shore, dumping him into the surf. They had not always been successful when they attempted to launch a surf boat in heavy seas. Occasionally the boat would capsize, dumping all hands into the icy water. After several unsuccessful attempts they would have to resort to the breeches buoy.

One of the more daring girls rides the breeches buoy during a drill at the Merrimack River Life Saving Station, c. 1910.

For years I had heard talk about the big fire but knew little about it except that everything on the curve (the bend in the tracks at the center), plus the Dance Pavilion had been destroyed by a fire in 1913. One day I questioned Uncle Tom about it and this is what he told me: He was coming along the shore from the Point toward the station on Thursday, July 9th, in midafternoon, with Inez and the Chariot, when suddenly he

40

Left: Merrimack River Station crew rigging a breeches buoy for drill, c. 1910. Plum Island lighthouse is visible in the background.

Photo below:
The original Dance Pavilion at Plum Island center, c. 1910.

saw great columns of smoke and red flames shooting skyward. He urged Inez to a trot and as he approached the station, he yelled for all hands on deck. His son Jay, who was in the tower had spotted the fire, alerting the others who were out front with all the buckets when he pulled up. With Jay and Ralph on the seat with him and all the buckets in the back, he took off for the fire. Bill, with three of the Wood boys, Ted, Ralph, and Leon, ran to jump on the trolley which was on it's way by. As he approached the center he could see that all the buildings on the curve, including Noyes' refreshment stand, were completely engulfed in flame, and Merril's store was beginning to burn. About this time the Pavilion, on the other side of the tracks, burst into flames in several places simultaneously. A crowd had gathered, some throwing sand on the flames, others beating frantically at the flames with brooms, the rest milling around in mass confusion. Inez was tied to a piazza post of the Chesley house. Horses get panicky in the presence of fire, so a large cloth was tied over her head so she could not see the flames. Uncle Tom noticed the wind was from the southwest and most of the burning embers were

blowing toward the shore. However, because there had been almost no rain since May, everything was tinder dry and threatened to catch fire just from the proximity of a building burning next door.

Knowing everyone well, as he did, Uncle Tom hailed owners of nearby cottages to bring others to help and every bucket they could find. Immediately he had his boys start a bucket brigade from a pump at the Green Davis place to wet down the Davis cottage. However, the ever increasing heat from the burning Pavilion was too much to bear. Moving to the other side of the house to the barn, they ran the brigade from the barn pump to the barn. By this time, dozens of buckets had been gathered and Uncle Tom had Bill and the Wood boys set up two more bucket brigades from the pumps at the cottages next to the barn. With these three brigades and using two ladders, they were able to keep the barn from igniting. Next Uncle Tom got the neighboring women to bring blankets and bedspreads, which were wetted and used to beat out any stray embers that reached adjacent cottages. When the Chesly cottage began to smolder, a bucket brigade was moved to wet that down. In a little over a half hour, the flames were pretty well spent. All the buildings on the curve were lost, as well as the Pavilion and the Green Davis cottage. The Davis barn and other cottages were saved.

A hose wagon and a ladder from Newburyport Central Fire Station arrived followed by Fire Chief Osborne in his own auto. They took over, allowing the fire to burn out under control, using hoses and chemicals. When everything was under control the Maddock and Wood boys plunged into the ocean, clothes and all, closely followed by dozens of others. All agreed it was the hottest fire they had ever seen.

The only things saved were the money draw from Merrill's Store along with a few cases of tonic. Also, all the musical instruments, with the exception of the piano, were

Plum Island center after the fire of 1913. The Davis barn and Chesly cottage are to the right of the tracks.

salvaged from the Pavilion. All the contents of the Chesley cottage were removed, but in such great haste that much of the furniture was badly damaged. Unfortunately so, for the cottage was only scorched.

Uncle Tom remembered a few men who were a big help to him that day: Roy Smith of Haverhill, and a Colonel Merrill from Boston, as well as George Gibbs. Most of all he praised the trolley motorman, Earl Delano. He was very positive that had it not been for the Maddock and Wood boys, many more cottages would have been lost. He also said he believed if the wind had been blowing a little more from the south, everything on the Island could have gone.

The trolley company sent down a gang of workers and before night-fall new poles were set, the wires were restrung, and the cars were running again. Everything had quieted down and people were enjoying the cool evening breeze when suddenly a little after dark, the Plum Island Bridge caught fire. The section between the draw and the Island was destroyed, cutting off the trolley service again. The trolley company quickly built a foot bridge over the river the next day, but it took most of the summer to rebuild the bridge. Meanwhile people rode the trolley from Newburyport to Plum Island River, walked across the foot bridge, then took a car on the other side to the Island. Some people used boats, while others took the Salisbury Ferry. Uncle Tom said the fire department blamed the careless disposal of cigarettes for both fires.

A year later, he told me, the Plum Island Hotel which stood near where Angie's gas station is now, burned. He told me there had been nothing anyone could do but wet down the car barn across the street. Its roof did catch fire, but the Newburyport Fire Department arrived in time to extinguish it.

The Plum Island Hotel in its heyday, c. 1910.
Angie's service station stands there today.

Looking down Plum Island River from High Sandy., c. 1910.
The Plum Island Hotel can be seen on the horizon in the center.

Another story was about the wreck of the Jennie M. Carter, out of Providence. Uncle Tom was not a witness to this, but it had been related to him by one of his crew members who had been at the station at that time.

Shortly after daybreak on Friday, April 13, 1894, while the station crew was at chow, the man in the tower spotted a three masted schooner foundering out front. A vicious storm was raging, with snow squalls and the schooner was not visible all the time because of the blowing snow. Her foresail, the only sail set, had two or three reefs. She was tossing to and fro about a half mile out, obviously out of control. A surf boat was quickly launched and taken out to the vessel, which proved to be the Jennie M. Carter hailing from Providence, Rhode Island. They were unable to board her because of the extremely heavy sea but there appeared to be no one on board. The life boat was gone and the davit was smashed, but they stood by just in case someone had remained on board. When she finally came to rest on the shore at Salisbury Beach, fifteen feet of her main mast was all that was left above deck, her jib boom was split off and her hull was badly damaged. About ten a.m. the station crew boarded her. They took all her papers, along with the barometer and quadrant, and left.

Right: Old octagonal lighthouse in 1897, shortly before being replaced by the present one. Black streaks were caused by soot from the kerosene lamp.

Previous page: A typical scene from the shore, c. 1892.

Below: The working mechanism of the Plum Island lighthouse lamp, 1896.

She had been sighted in trouble by another ship a couple of days earlier and were urged to abandon ship for two hours. The six man crew, clinging to the rigging, refused to leave the ship and that was the last that was seen of them. By noon because of the wretched shape the hull was in, the authorities were predicting the schooner would be broken up during the extra high tide expected that afternoon, however, due to the weight of her cargo, which was stone, she remained solid in the sand for years. Indeed, I recall seeing her remains there in the early thirties. Uncle Tom said, being the superstitious lot they were, all the seafaring men in the area blamed the wreck on it occurring on Friday the thirteenth.

47

I went on many hikes around the Island with not only Uncle Tom, but with my father and grandfather. Sometimes we would all go together and were occasionally joined by Uncle Ted. On one hike we went down to the south end to Grape Island, where they showed me the posts in the ground and part of the first floor of what had once been a hotel. Another time we went to Bar Head, where there had once been a key post, and around Sandy Point up the Plum Island River shore to where there stood several abandoned cottages. The owners had been forced out when the government took over that part of the Island, I was told. Several times we searched unsuccessfully for a sea gull rookery which my grandfather remembered seeing as a boy. Also, a legendary shell mound, supposedly created by the American Indians who came to Plum Island for games and to feast on clams and fish, was sought in vain. We visited the Polio Camp, formerly the Knobbs Life Saving Station.

Wharf to the hotel at Plum Island Bluffs, c. 1895.

Uncle Tom told me how the northern end of the Island had been formed. Several winter storms in succession in 1839 had cut through the end of Salisbury Beach creating an island. During the next ten or so years it was gradually washed away and deposited on the northern end of Plum Island, then located about where the church now stands. This became a narrow sand spit reaching northward until it was nearly even with what was then Plum Island point; now called Old Point, forming the Basin.

48

Around 1883 the south jetty was built parallel to the north jetty on the Salisbury side of the river, which had been built two years previously. These jetties were expected to keep sand bars from forming in the mouth of the river. At about the same time, fearing the Merrimack River would revert to the original mouth, a rubble stone dike was placed across the mouth of the Basin.

One day Uncle Tom took me to a spot at the seaward side of the road in line with what was then the Patience House. He pointed out a few rocks by the side of the road, and stooping to scoop out more sand revealed many more rocks. "This is the spot where the jetty begins." he informed me. This spot is now located on the corner lot at Northern Boulevard and Sixty-Third Street. No rocks are visible today. We walked in the direction of the ocean, and when we reached an area opposite the rear of the Patience House, the rocks became visible again. The further we went, the more the rocks protruded above the sand. As we approached the Coast Guard Station, the rocks

From the lookout tower of the Merrimack River Life Saving Station, c. 1910. Plum Island basin is in the background. The cottage on the right with the dark roof is the Rinkoo-Tei.

disappeared into the sand again. Out in front of the station the rocks once again were well above the sand as they went into the water. "That spot, at the edge of the road, was where the edge of the shore was when the jetty was built." Uncle Tom told me, "All this sand between the point and here and out in front of the Coast Guard Station was caught and held by the jetty. It continued to be built up higher and further north by the action of the wind and water until it became as it is now. The beach grass held it in place."

Periodically the jetty was extended as the beach pushed out further and further.

When it was extended in 1932 it was done at an angle southward. After that, each time there was a storm and an unusually high tide, the beach opposite the head of the Basin would wash away a little more. By 1945 there was very little beach between the cottages and the ocean. Twice during winter storms of that period I remember waves washing over the porches on both sides of the Elora cottage and continuing out to the road. It was thought by many at that time that indeed, the ocean was going to cut through and join the Basin at precisely the same spot that used to be the mouth of the Merrimack River.

In the 1940's, at the time of the erosion on the shore opposite the church, there was a high knoll upon which stood a cottage owned by a doctor. As the beach eroded in

Groveland Ladies Aid Society at the Elora cottage on Plum Island, c. 1905.

Mary Worthen is at the far left, Mrs. Bert Waldow, owner of the cottage next door, is beside her with her son Hollis at her feet.

front of it, the doctor would have the cottage moved back toward the road, where it remains today. Each time he moved it he had to purchase another lot of land. Fortunately, he had the money to pay for it. Other cottage owners soon followed suit. But eventually, due to a lack of funds or available land, all of the cottages were not moved far enough. Between 1946 and 1948 several cottages were lost to the sea. It was tragic to see the owners standing helplessly as successive waves ate away more and more sand until the cottage pitched forward and in a matter of minutes, slid into the sea.

Above: Plum Island Point from across the basin.
The original Old Point Road is in the foreground.

Below: Plum Island Point from the station lookout tower, c. 1910.

The waves would quickly break it up and wash it away scattering the contents. In what seemed no time at all, there would be nothing left but a few boards and other debris. By the next day, all that remained to show there had been a cottage there was a few cedar posts and a pitcher pump atop a bent well pipe. As I watched this occur, I could not help but reflect what Uncle Tom had told me the day he showed me the base of the jetty. "They should be very careful how they add on to the end of the jetty", he stated solemnly. "Each time they change the direction of the jetty, it will alter the erosion pattern and the beach will be eaten away in a different place. It could put many cottages in danger". He had prophesied what would happen and was right.

Many courses of action were taken to stop the erosion, such as hydraulic dredging of sand from the basin to discharge it along the shore in the most seriously depleted areas, but it did not take more than a couple of years for the sea to remove it all again. The situation did aid boaters in the basin by creating a deeper channel but this did not last either, as it gradually filled back in over the next few years.

Another project was the construction of rock groins along the shore at intervals of

Frank Worthen placing a For Sale sign on his old Grand Banks dory, after purchasing a new one in Amesbury, from Lowell's Boat Shop, c.1918.

about five hundred yards. These little jetties were carefully laid by a stone mason with the help of a crane. They extended from the shore about a hundred feet. The sand built on them immediately, and for a while the beach filled in on the north side of each groin. It appeared to be a success until 1954 when Hurricane Carol scattered those big heavy rocks as though they were pebbles. At the same time it blew away, piece by piece, the Pavilion at the Center, and toppled my cottage the "Sheridan", on Sixteenth Street. The Sheridan ended up flat on the sand at a 30 degree list. It took me a week with the help of two railroad jacks to right it and get posts under it. The Sheridan was one of the Barker cottages carrying Albert Barker's middle name, coincidentally, it was also my wife, Hope's, maiden name. My sister Marjorie bought it from Albert in 1942 and sold it to my mother and father, and my wife and me in 1953. To me, the real tragedy of that incident was the loss of my Old town canoe which I had spent the summer patching and painting. Only a few days previously my father and I had placed it under the cottage for the winter, after having taken it out on the Basin to check it for leaks. It was as flat as a pancake!

In 1960 the jetty was extended again and the beach, where the cottages had washed out, began to build up once more. It continued to fill in until it extended further out than anyone could recall. However, the bad news was erosion up toward High Sandy, and on the shore of the river in front of the Coast Guard Station to a point where it became necessary to demolish it and replace it with a facility up in Newburyport.

The Basin cottage, Plum Island, c. 1905.

53

With the exception of his son Ralph and family, I have scanty recollection of any other of Uncle Tom's family. Richie, I knew was in the Navy but I can't recall what he did after that. I do remember one story about Richie. While in Manila Bay in the Philippines, the flag ship with Admiral Dewey on board, was passing Richie's ship. As was the custom, all hands were on deck at salute, as the Admiral passed by. It seems Richie was trying so hard to get a glimpse of the Admiral, he fell over the side into the water between ships. After being rescued, he faced Captain's Mast and was disciplined for his inappropriate action. I also remember that Richie died at a fairly young age.

Jay also died quite young. Willard and his family lived in Salem, New Hampshire. He was at the Bonnyview cottage occasionally when I was a boy. Ruth married Walter Lothrop and moved to Plainsville, Connecticut. I only remember seeing her a few times. John lived with his mother on Main Street, in Groveland, Massachusetts when I was a boy. Ralph married Bessie Hopkinson from Groveland. She and her sister, Sarah, inherited the Hopkinson Farm in Groveland. Ralph and his brother-in-law, Vernon Talton, called it Valley Farm and operated it as a dairy farm quite successfully for many years. They had over sixty herd of cattle, both Jersey and Guernsey. I recall Ralph once saying "Guernsey for quantity, and Jersey for quality." The farm was situated in the Savoryville section of Groveland and embraced many acres of land between Main Street and the Merrimack River all along the bank at Flannigan's Bend as far as the West Newbury town line.

In grammar school, I became friendly with Ralph's son Griffith. Grif was a year older than I, but because of the closeness of our families, we became good friends.

The steamer, Merrimack, which made regular runs between Haverhill and Plum island Point, passing through the Groveland bridge draw, c. 1900.

He would take me home with him after school; I was intrigued with farm life. I spent many Saturdays with Grif at the farm for a few years. He always had chores to do and I enjoyed helping him. I loved life at the farm among the cows, horses, pigs, and chickens. I suppose, with my grandfather Wood being the ninth generation of farmers in Groveland, it was in my blood. I was always invited to join the family at dinner and I loved farm-grown food. I learned to feed the animals, milk cows, harness the horse to a wagon, to plow, and to ride horseback. Grif and Ruth had a pony named "Merrylegs". Because of the demanding life of the farm, Ralph and his family, although owning a cottage at the Island, had little chance to enjoy it fully. Every member of their family had many chores to do. A farm with all those animals needed attention twenty four hours a day. Grif told me on more than one occasion, he wished he could spend more time with his grandfather.

Grif had a sister three years older than he, named Ruth, after Ralph's sister. They called her Becky. She was a very pretty girl, but at that age she seemed very grown up to me, so I did not get to know her very well. She became a school teacher, and taught for years at Groveland High School. She is married to John Adams and at this writing resides in Harwich Port, Massachusetts.

As we grew older, my interests changed and Grif was unable to participate in many of my activities because he was needed on the farm. We grew apart, however we did double date with girls quite often when in our late teens. Valley Farm supplied milk and eggs to most of the residents of the town. When Ralph died, Grif inherited his share of the farm and operated it until his death, in the late eighties. He was a man of sterling character and inherited a lot of his grandfather's wit and humor.

The last picture of the steamer Merrimack. It is shown above sinking after striking a rock in the Merrimack River near Rocks Village.

Sketch of Wishbone

`About the same time the first road was built, a whale washed ashore at Salisbury Beach. Uncle Tom, enlisting the help of some of the boys from the station, went to Salisbury Beach. They removed a vertebra from the backbone of the whale with the two ribs still attached. They brought it to Plum Island where it was set up with the ends of the ribs set in concrete, one on each side of the walkway to the Bonnyview. It formed an arch over the walk which resembled a huge wishbone. It was named "Captain Maddock's Wishbone" by the people of the Island. A cottage, located beside the Bonnyview and directly behind the wishbone, which belonged to Uncle Tom's son, Ralph, was named "The Wishbone". It stood like that for nearly fifty years, until the ends of the ribs in the concrete deteriorated and were crumbling so that it became unsafe and was removed.

One Saturday morning in July when I was nine or ten years old, my father asked if I would like to go up in the lighthouse. Of course, the answer was in the affirmative. I was very excited and could not wait to get started. We walked to the Bonnyview, where it seemed we were expected. After what seemed an eternity, with Dad talking to Uncle Tom and Aunt Alice, Uncle Tom said it was time to go. He must have made arrangements for us to be there at a certain time. We walked to the lighthouse. It had

Plum Island lighthouse just after being erected in 1897.

never seemed as far before. The door of the light keeper's house was opened by a man introduced to me by Uncle Tom as Mr. Kezer. "So this is the young man who wants to go up to see the light," said Mr. Kezer. "Yes sir!" I hastened to answer.

We went next door to the lighthouse. It seemed much bigger as we got close to it. Mr. Kezer opened the door and we followed him inside, up the stairs around and around.... a long way to the top. On the landing at the top, the light appeared huge to me. Around and around it went, never stopping. Two bright flashes went by every few seconds, one long, and one short. Morse code for the letter N, denoting Newburyport.

Top photo: Surf boat drill in progress off Plum Island, c. 1909.
Bottom photo: Butler's Toothpick, Black Rocks, Salisbury, c. 1905.
Fishermen in a Grand Banks dory to left.

57

The mechanism looked very complicated. Mr. Kezer told me that before the electric light had been put in about five years before, the light had been created by a big kerosene lamp

Looking out the windows the view was impressive from all sides. I could look out over everything. Mr. Kezer, Uncle Tom, and Dad all had favorite landmarks to point out in every direction. Not only sites on Plum Island, but also in the river, over in Salisbury, and up in Newburyport: the bell buoy, the whistler, cottages, boats, church steeples, etc. What fascinated me most, I believe, was the bright red, pyramid shaped object over near the shore at Black Rocks, Salisbury. They called it "Butler's Toothpick" and it was a navigation aid for boats coming in the mouth of the river. I wish I could remember all the stories they told about it; I found them very interesting at the time. As we left I thanked Mr. Kezer for showing me the light. We went to Hynes' Store across the road down towards the point. I loved inspecting all the things for sale in there: kites, sail boats, toys, etc. Dad bought us each a donut which we ate as we walked over to the

Captain Thomas J. Maddock and unidentified crew members.

Coast Guard Station. Both Uncle Tom and Dad were well known at the station. The crew was just sitting down to noon chow and we were invited to join them. I thoroughly enjoyed the mashed potato, string beans, and braised beef. For dessert they served chocolate cake & milk. The men all made a lot of me, showing me the boats and equipment out in the garages. They told me they had a big motor boat at the boat house over at the point. They said they took it out every day for a short ride to see if everything was working all right. I asked if I could have a ride. They told me if I was around when they went out I could. When we got back to the station, Uncle Tom and Dad were ready to leave but they waited while the men took me up in the tower. I could see almost everything that I had seen in the lighthouse, and even more of what was out to sea with a pair of binoculars.

Right after breakfast on Monday morning, telling my mother I was going to visit Uncle Tom, I made straight for the Point. The Coast Guard patrol boat was tied up at the wharf in front of the boat house. I sat in the sand near the boat house door. I did not care if I had to wait there all day, I was bound and determined to be present when they took the boat out.

Lady Luck was with me for in about a half hour, two of the crew came. They recognized me and knew I was there for the promised ride. Everything was ready to go, the way they always kept it in case of an emergency. The men strapped a life jacket on me, then donned them themselves. The life jackets were made of canvas with compartments containing strips of cork running from top to bottom. It was far too big for me but regulations specified I must wear it. It was so big and stiff, it was rather difficult for me to sit.

Merrimack River Station, c. 1905. Capt. Maddock on left.

59

The big engine started with a roar, we cast off and were on our way. I jerked backward as the boat surged ahead. I had never been in a boat that went that fast and I was thrilled. We went up river a short way, then turned in the direction of the sea. We passed by the Toothpick so close I could see through the boards that covered it. It had looked much smoother from the lighthouse even through the binoculars. It also appeared much larger close up. In no time we were passing through the rough water over the bar at the mouth of the river. A big spray flew back on both sides and the boat twisted and turned until we crossed the bar. I felt a little apprehensive, but the crewmen seemed unconcerned. We went around the north jetty and along the Salisbury shore a little way, then we came about and returned. On the way in, over the bar, it was a smoother ride. The boat twisted from side to side and we kept surging ahead again and again. Back at the wharf, we tied up and everything was secured once again in readiness for a quick get away. I thanked the men and walked to the Bonnyview where I excitedly related my experience to Uncle Tom. He told me they needed the fast boat more for chasing the rum runners, who, more and more, were attempting to smuggle liquor up the river and on to isolated spots on the Island. The only part of the boat trip I didn't like was how quickly it ended.

Twice each fall, while I was growing up, there was a family excursion to the south end of Plum Island, once to pick beach plums on the first weekend in September, and

Cottage beside the hotel at Plum Island Bluffs c. 1895

again a couple of weeks later to gather cranberries. My grandfather and grandmother Wood, Uncle Ted and his family, my father and his family, all met at the Elora, then walked down the shore to High Sandy. There we made our way inland through the dunes to find the plum bushes. The plum bushes were everywhere all the way to the Bluffs, though we seldom went more than a mile or so before our containers were full. Unfortunately poison ivy was everywhere also. Everyone scrubbed down with yellow laundry soap when we returned to the cottage. If you knew you had been exposed to poison ivy, and used the yellow laundry soap, there was little likelihood of being affected; at least it worked that way for us. Everyone had a picking can. A picking can was made by punching two holes on opposite sides of a tin can near the top. A string was tied at each end to the holes. The can was hung around the neck and adjusted to a comfortable position so it was easy to drop the plums in. Each family had two large kettles into which the individual cans were dumped when they were full.

During the years of my recollection, there was sometimes a baby. First, my sister Dorothy, then Uncle Ted's son, Kenneth. My sister Elizabeth was the last I remember, for by the time my brother David was born, we no longer went as a group. Lois and I were the same age. My sister Marjorie was two years younger, while my brother Richard was five years younger.

Two barrel staves nailed to the bottom of a good sized wooden box, made a sleigh in which to pull the babies over the sand. The box held a pillow for a mattress and had a rope with which to pull it. Little shelters were made with blankets to keep the sun off the babies. The grown-ups would take turns watching the babies. Small children were paired up with older children so they would not get lost and everyone stayed pretty much together as we picked. Each family also brought their own picnic basket. At noon we would gather together to eat lunch. Early in the afternoon, the kettles would be full and we would walk back to the Elora. The rest of the day would be spent swimming and relaxing on the beach or on the piazza.

Cranberry bogs were located in the vicinity of High Sandy and this trip was pretty much the same as the plum picking, however everyone stayed together picking cranberries. The cranberries grew close to the ground so we were forced to squat down or crawl on our hands and knees to pick. Again individual cans were around our necks, but instead of kettles we had large canvas sacks to contain the cranberries. As soon as all the berries were picked in one bog, we would move on to another. Our bags were usually full while we were still in the third bog. The grown-ups and older children would take turns carrying the bags on on the way back. Jelly was made from the plums and cranberry sauce was made from the cranberries. Sometimes there would be some of each left well into the next summer.

In the fall of every year, all the boats belonging to cottage owners were taken from the water and hauled well above the high water mark on to the basin shore where they were turned upside down. In the spring all the seams which had opened up as the wood dried out during the winter, were filled with a cotton yarn called caulking. The caulking was packed tight with a tool called a caulking iron. It resembled a broad chisel but instead of a sharp blade it had a flat edge about an eighth of an inch thick and was slightly curved. Then the boat was painted and put in the water. It was filled, to the gunwales, with water and allowed to swell for a few days. As the planks swelled, they pushed together holding the caulking firmly in place.

One year when I was ten or eleven years old, due to a series of rainy weekends we were very late getting our dory into the water. My father and Uncle Ted planned a fishing trip for a Sunday in mid June. It turned out to be the same weekend the boat was to be put in the water. My father took the clam digger out on the flats before the tide came in Saturday morning. Turning over the muck with the digger, again and again, ignoring the clams he quickly tossed big fat worm after worm out for me to pick up and place in the can. When the can was full he brought it into the shore where he dumped the worms spreading them around in the dry sand. He explained that the worms would stay alive, and livelier, coated with sand. Wet seaweed was placed in the bottom of the wooden worm box. Next the worms, then another layer of wet seaweed on top. The worms were kept overnight in the ice chest up at the cottage, assuring a good supply of fresh, lively bait for the next day. The boat was put in the water and filled as soon as the tide came in.

That afternoon, taking out the basket of fishing tackle, my father checked over the lines. Line deteriorated during the winter so it was necessary to see if it was strong enough to hold a good-sized, active fish. Starting at one end, Dad would wrap the line around each hand with a couple of feet in between, and give it a sharp snap. If it broke any place at all, the whole line would be thrown out, for if it broke with a fish on it, not

only the fish would be lost, but also the lead sinker. Sinkers were made by pouring melted lead into a four inch cylindrical mold about an inch thick, formed in the wet sand. An eight penny nail was cast into each end to be removed after the sinker was cooled. The holes left by the nails were used to attach one end to the line and the other to an eighteen inch piece of line, called a leader, which held the fish hook. A more elaborate sinker known as a spreader, was made by casting a twelve inch length of 1/8" brass rod through the lead in place of the bottom nail. The rod was bent into a small ring at each end. Each of these rings held a leader with a hook. With a spreader it was possible and quite common to catch two fish at the same time if a school of fish passed by.

A hard wood fire burned down to a bed of white hot coals was used to melt the lead in a cast iron melting pot. When the lead became molten, scale was skimmed from the surface and a cast iron ladle was used to dip it out to pour into the mold. It hardened almost immediately but took quite a while to become cool enough to handle. With the lines checked, the tackle was stowed in the basket. All was ready but the boat. Dad was worried it would not swell enough in one day to be sea worthy. When we emptied the boat and took it out early Sunday morning it leaked badly. "I knew it hadn't been in the water long enough!" my father declared. "We can't take that outside." he continued. "We'll have to get a boat from Albert Barker." The boat was put back in the water and filled again. We walked down the basin shore almost to the Point, to a grey cottage beside a big grey boat house where many pale green grand bank dories lined the shore. On the bow of each, in black letters. was printed "A.S. BARKER" with a number.

We were met at the door by a very pleasant man whom Dad respectfully addressed as "Mr. Barker". "Hello, Ralph," said Mr. Barker, "What brings you around so early in the morning?" After my father explained our situation and informed him we wished to rent

Plum Island Point taken from the river mouth side, c. 1910.

63

The Dike cottage at the entrance to Plum Island basin. The rocks at the end of the dike are visible in the foreground, c. 1910.

one of his dories, he graciously told Dad he could not rent one, but he could borrow it. (I believe the going price for a boat rental, at that time, was fifteen cents an hour.) Dad thanked him as we accompanied him next door to the boat house where he gave us two sets of oars and oar locks which we placed in the boat. After some small talk, during which Mr. Barker commented that soon I would be as tall as my father, we walked back to the cottage, getting there just before Uncle Ted and Grandpa Wood arrived. Taking the fishing tackle basket, bait box, lunch basket, and a small tub to hold the fish, we walked to the Bonnyview, where Uncle Tom told us he would not be able to go, as he had company coming from Concord.

We walked to the boat and waited for the tide to come in enough to get the boat over the dike into the harbor. The dike, in those days was in fairly good condition, a solid dam of rocks from shore to shore. Half way across was a section of about twenty five or more feet which was between three and four feet lower than the rest. At full high tide, the entire dike was covered with water. At dead low tide, the water level on the basin side was slightly below the height of the sluiceway, while on the harborside, the entire structure of the dike was visible. When the water began to run back in over the sluiceway, the velocity increased rapidly to a point where it was very difficult to get a boat through the opening. It was advisable to work the boat over to the other side as quickly as possible, for if the current became too strong, it would be necessary to wait

Helen Wood sitting on the whistling buoy, which was washed ashore at Plum Island in a storm, c. 1908. Her mother, Jennie Maddock Wood, is sitting behind the buoy.

nearly an hour before the boat could be rowed over. The boat was taken over to the opening. Then all hands, with pants rolled to the knees, climbed out onto the rocks on both sides and worked the boat over. They pulled it around to the high part of the dike. Back in the boat it could now be rowed out into the river.

The Coast Guard was very strict about the condition of their life preservers and as soon as they showed any fraying or deterioration they were surveyed, (discarded). These surveyed preservers were still useful for many years and we had a few in the boat.

With Dad and Uncle Ted both rowing we made good headway against the morning tide, until we reached the area where the north and south jetty were not too far apart. There the current was so strong it seemed that sometimes you would move ahead two feet, then fall back eight. Reaching the turbulent water over the sand bar at the mouth of the river. we literally had to fight our way through. It was very difficult to keep the boat headed straight on because the water was full of whirlpools and waves from opposing directions. The further out we got, the easier it became, until finally, in the open sea, we made good headway.

It was so calm they decided to go all the way out to the "Whistler" (the whistling buoy which marked the channel three miles out. It whistled so that it could be located in the fog.) As we passed near the bell buoy, I was amazed how loud the clanging was. This was my first time out except for my ride in the Coast guard boat, and I had never heard the bell buoy other than from shore. Aboard the Coast Guard boat, the engine made so much noise I could not hear anything else. When we reached our destination I was again surprised at the sound of the "Whistler" from only a few feet away. The soft moaning sound I had become accustomed to, the sound that lulled me to sleep as I lay in bed at night, was now like the blast of a steam ship horn.

After throwing out the anchor and giving the line enough scope to hold in the sandy bottom, we got down to the business of fishing for flounder. Dad sat in the stern, Grampa and Uncle Ted sat at the sides, with me in the bow: trying to keep my line from becoming tangled in the anchor line that remained in the boat. We must have fished for an hour or more, catching no more than an occasional skulpin or silver hake, which of course, were thrown back. There was much discussion about whether or not we should try another location. Suddenly everyone had a flounder on his line. Dad and Uncle Ted were pulling them in two at a time. As fast as their hooks could be baited and put over the side, they had another fish. Soon the small galvanized tub we brought to hold the catch had over three dozen fish in it. That was plenty so we hauled anchor and went in. The tide was not quite full as we reached home.

The grown ups dressed the fish right on the basin shore while I watched. Each one found a small piece of board, of which there were many scattered along the high water

The Barker cottage and boathouse, Plum Island, c. 1905. Both buildings are still standing but greatly altered. An addition on the cottage and the boathouse has been converted to an apartment house. Located at the end of 76th Street.

mark. Then they proceeded, first to cut off the fish's head, then slit the belly to remove the guts. They cut through the skin along the edges on both back and belly at the place where the meat met the fins. Lifting the edge of the skin at the head end and using plenty of dry sand to hold the slippery fish, the skin was pulled from the fish both back and belly. Finally, with razor-sharp knives, the meat was cleanly skived from the bones in four pieces. There were now over twelve dozen fillets of black back flounder. Black back flounder are native to the waters of the Plum Island area. They differ from the yellow tail in that the meat of the back is filled with little blue-black flecks and they have a particular flavor all their own. The fillets were washed in the basin, then taken to the cottage to be washed again thoroughly with clean, fresh water. As soon as we moved away, the noisy sea gulls that had been circling overhead all the while, swooped down to clean up the leavings, squawking as they fought over the feast. Uncle Ted and Grandpa left soon after the cleaned fish were divided.

I went with Dad as he rowed the boat back to Barker's. Mr. Barker thanked me as he gratefully accepted one of the two packages of fish my mother had handed me as

Albert Sheridan Barker standing by his cottage at Plum Island, c. 1905.

67

I left the cottage. Uncle Tom was equally pleased when I gave him the other package on the way by. I was curious about Mr. Barker, and knowing he and Uncle Tom were very good friends, I went down to the Bonnyview to see what I could learn from him. He told me Albert Sheridan Barker, a young man living in Groveland in the 1890's had been hurt on the job, and after receiving a sizable cash settlement, he had decided to invest it by building a few beach cottages at Plum Island. His venture had proved very successful and his cottages were easily rented all summer. He kept reinvesting the proceeds in more cottages in various places all over the Island from the Point to the Center, both in Newburyport and Newbury. By the period before World War II he had about forty cottages. They were all furnished simply but adequately and some included the use of a Grand Banks dory. The porch furniture included several of the porch rockers, popular even now, with broad arms and woven reed seats and backs, made by a company in South Carolina. The cottages were painted white with green trim. The interiors were painted pale green. They all had a name plaque attached to the front. All the cottages had piazzas at the front and some had piazzas on all four sides. There was a back house privy behind each cottage. Some of the cottages were rented for the entire season from April 15th to October 15th, during the time the water pumps could safely operate without freezing. Every cottage was named. At first he chose family names such as Albert and Sheridan, his first and middle names. Then Charles and Alice after his son and daughter-in-law, and Dorothy, for his granddaughter. Others included: George, Sumner, Edith, Elizabeth, and many others.

Albert also bought Grand Banks dories from Lowell's boat shop in Amesbury. Those that didn't go with a cottage were available for rent by anyone. He also built a large boat house in which the boats, oars and oar locks were stored for winter. Equipment and supplies used to handle and maintain the boats and the cottages were in there also. Albert Barker was very enterprising, and in addition to the cottages and boats, he also sold ice and kerosene.

When I was a young man in Groveland, Albert's son Charles operated a fuel oil business. He was one of the first to take oil from house to house in a tank truck. During the nineteen forties, when Albert reached the age when he needed help running his business, Alice Barker, the widow of his son Charles, came to live with him and take care of what he was unable to do himself. After his death, Alice took over the business. Alice was a lovely lady; quick to help anyone in need. Energetic and hard working, she was respected and loved by all who knew her. And, because she was as enterprising as her father-in-law, the business prospered under her hand. In later years, her grand-daughter Alice, her daughter Dorothy's daughter, came to stay with her and eventually the business became hers.

I recall a trip up Plum Island River somewhere around 1933. Uncle Ted brought his outboard motor and affixed it to the stern piece of our Grand Banks dory. It was a bright sunny day in July as we caught the morning tide. Uncle Ted was at the helm, my father, my grandfather, Uncle Tom, and myself were aboard, along with a large picnic basket.

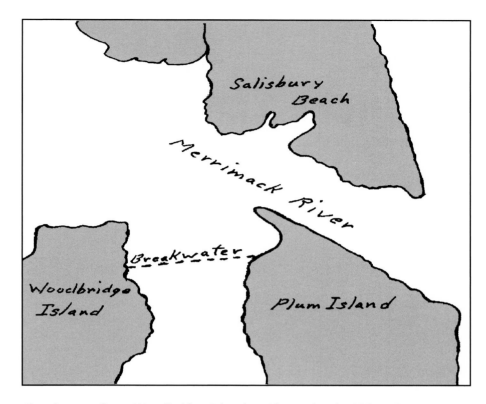

Breakwater from Woodbridge Island to Plum Island 1829 - 1831.

We proceeded up Plum Island River, stopping now and then to look at objects of interest At some point we reached a place where the incoming tide from the Merrimack River and the incoming tide from Ipswich Bay met, in opposition to each other. It formed a visible ridge of water across the river and caused the motor to run unevenly for a moment.

After crossing the tide divide, we continued to Sandy Point where we went ashore to eat our picnic lunch. Here the sand was more white and fine than the coarse brown sand of Plum Island Beach. We swam and sat on the beach in the sunshine. By the time we started back, the tide was well on it's way out. We went from Plum Island River into the Merrimack, passing between Woodbridge and Plum Island. Uncle Tom and Grandpa Wood both warned Uncle Ted to be careful not to strike the motor on the rocks as we passed over the breakwater. Because I was riding in the bow, I was designated to watch for the breakwater. "I see it! I see it!" I shouted as I spied a ridge of rocks directly in front of us near the water's surface. Uncle Ted stopped the engine and barely had the outboard tilted back before we were upon the rocks. My father and I jumped from the boat just in time to prevent it from striking the breakwater. Everyone got out of the boat and with the help of the swiftly moving, outgoing tide we lifted the dory over the breakwater. Back in the boat with the engine running, we quickly made our way toward the basin.

Everyone agreed we would be lucky to get the boat into the basin against the rush of the water over the dike. When we reached the basin, the top of the dike showed above the water, and the opening in the middle was filled with outflowing water of unbelievable velocity. Uncle Ted ran the engine at full throttle heading for the opening. As the boat started through the sluice-way, the rush of water nearly brought it to a standstill. Luckily we had enough momentum to carry us all the way through. Everyone heaved a sigh of relief as we continued up the basin.

On the way I questioned them about the breakwater. Uncle Tom explained how somewhere around 1830 it was decided to build a breakwater between the Plum Island Point, which is now Old Point, and Woodbridge Island. It was believed that slowing the flow of water going out between Woodbridge Island and the Point would allow less sand to be washed into the mouth of the Merrimack River, thus preserving a deeper, clearer channel through the mouth. Unfortunately, after all the work and expense, it made no

The Rinkoo-Tei cottage, Plum Island, c. 1905.
"The place between the waters." So named by
a visiting Japanese dignitary.

70

appreciable difference. They still had to dredge the mouth of the river every few years. The dredger was a ship with a crane, equipped with a clam shell-like device at the end of a cable. The clam shell would be dropped into the water in an open position. As it was pulled up, it would close, filling with sand. The sand would be dumped onto barges which were then taken to Boston where the sand was used as aggregate in the mixing of concrete, or taken out to deep water and dumped overboard.

The water taken from driven wells on Plum Island were noted for their clear purity. It was possible to drive a well almost anywhere and get good water. Sometime in May every year, my father would put new leather washers in the pitcher pump at the Elora cottage. Holding his hand over the spout, he would prime the pump by pouring water into the top of the pump. His hand would keep the water in while he gave the handle a few quick strokes. Soon water would pour from the pump with every stroke. At first it would be rusty from being idle all winter. Dad would keep pumping until the water

The Crescent cottage, Plum Island, c. 1893.
Second from left on the piazza is Frank M. Worthen from Groveland,
the author's maternal grandfather. On the extreme right is
Mary Worthen, holding Marian, the author's mother.

71

came clear. We children would all beg for the first tumblerfull to drink. In 1926 it was my turn to have the first drink. I started to gulp it down but quickly stopped and spit it out. "It tastes salty!" I told Dad. After sampling it himself, he informed me it was brackish. I insisted it was salty, not knowing they were one and the same.

Dad told Uncle Tom about the water. who attributed it to many exceptionally high tides throughout the winter. The sea had washed all around the cottage so many times it had seeped down into the water-table. He thought it might improve if a new point was driven, and only driven three feet below the top of the water table. They tried this and it was better, but not as good as it had been in the past. The next year it was worse and eventually, within a few years there was little difference between the well water and seawater.

We were not alone. All the wells in that section were the same. After the erosion of the forties there were almost no wells from the head of the basin to the Newburyport line along the shore that were not brackish. All drinking water had to be brought from other locations. We got ours from the Bonnyview. The situation became so acute, the City of Newburyport installed a faucet on the fire hydrant at the Sportsman's Lodge for Islanders to fill their jugs on the way down to Plum Island.

As I grew older and more busy with my social life, my visits to Uncle Tom became less frequent. I did not see him more than a half dozen times a year in the last few years before World War II. At one point he asked if I would be interested in attending the Coast Guard Academy. As a retired officer, he could get me an appointment and none of his grandchildren were interested. I was delighted and he put my name in. I went to Constitution Wharf in Boston, which was U.S. Coast Guard Headquarters, to take the

The Wosumonk cottage, Plum Island, c. 1905.

physical. I did not pass because I was missing some molars. I think, probably, Uncle Tom may have been even more disappointed than I.

Sometime in the early thirties he and Aunt Alice stopped staying on the Island during the winter months. They rented an apartment in Newburyport. "Getting too old to put up with these winter storms." Uncle Tom had said. I had not noticed that he was aging, but after I joined the Navy in 1941 and did not see him for over two years I saw the change in him. He was hale, hearty and still had his sharp wit and the twinkle in his eye, but his hair was very grey and he was a little stooped. I always stopped to see Uncle Tom when I was home on leave, but on July 6, 1945 I arrived home on leave to learn Uncle Tom had died on the fourth of July. My last visit with him was at the McKinney Funeral Home, at 124 High Street, Newburyport. He was laid out in full dress blue uniform in a flag-draped casket. He was almost eighty seven years old. He was buried in West Concord, New Hampshire

Maddock siblings c. 1919.
Left to right: Thomas, Jennie, Laura, and Alonzo.

Besides his wife Alice, Captain Maddock was survived by three sons, Willard, Ralph, and John, his daughter, Mrs. Walter Lothrop, two sisters; Mrs. Roswell Wood (Jennie), Mrs. Gardner Wood (Laura), eight grandchildren, of whom I only knew Ralph's children, Ruth and Griffith, and five great grandchildren.

Captain Thomas J. Maddock was an officer and a gentleman in the United States Life Saving Service. He was a caring and helpful person, and I loved him as my Uncle Tom.

On the back porch of the station, c. 1912. Left to right in front, Arthur Ellis, Laura Mae Wood Ellis, Helen Wood MacSpadden, unidentified person, John MacSpadden, Tom Wood (son of Jennie), Minerva Wood. Rear, Florence Maddock, Tom Maddock, and Jennie Maddock Wood.

The Seagull cottage, Plum Island, c. 1905.

Edith cottage, one of Barker's cottages, Plum Island, c. 1905.

A Grand Banks dory at the head of Plum Island basin looking toward the point, c. 1910.
Notice the tracks of Inez, the horse, and the Chariot in the sand.

The Genesta cottage Plum Island, which is still standing on 53rd Street, c. 1905.

Another of Barker's cottages, the Charles, Plum Island, c. 1905.

Above: The Maplewood cottage, Plum Island, c. 1905. Friends of cottage owners would often spend the weekend, helping to work on it.

Below: Highland cottage, Plum Island

Above: Hermitage cottage, Plum Island

Below: Massasoit Wigwam cottage, Plum Island, c. 1905.

*The
Seabreeze
cottage,
Plum
Island,
c. 1905,
owned by
H. E. Wales
of Haverhill.*

The Minnie E. cottage on basin shore, Plum Island, c. 1910.

81